AUTOPHAGY

How to Activate your Body and let it Purify
through Water Fasting, Intermittent Fasting,
Keto Diet to Lose Weight, Detox your Body,
Increase Muscle Mass, Slow Down Aging,
Stay Healthy.

TOSHIMORI YOICHI,
MARK DANIEL COOKSEY

Table of Contents

Introduction

This book is about autophagy, which is a gesture or process, in which individuals fast. The individuals that fast they observe marvelous qualities of smartness and agility in them and with the passage of time, the body makes them a big way of combating things. Combating things means that the body is able to endure a lot of pressure while in managerial works and the brain is able to make things look way better than the previous. The book will deal with many aspects of autophagy. What are the qualitative foods that define the working of food and how the activities or daily routine make the working of the body look more effective? The use and routine of autophagy through the intake of diets and how the public is able to get into proper shape will also be contextualized. The use of managerial ways and tactics through which autophagy is easily induced in the body and every deduction that can be affected with time. Therefore, the concept of autophagy and the inter-related concepts of autophagy will be elucidated in this book.

Autophagy can be used to describe a lot of benefits for the people. There are many uses of it. It can be used to cater to skin problems, it can give better improvisations for cancer-related patients, it can give a firm character building by expunging the bad diet from the body, it can also be used to reduce the risk of neuro-related diseases. Autophagy is also a way to make the body level reach the acme of strong blood pressure and all those heart-related diseases are also eliminated through it. Therefore, autophagy has many uses in this regard.

Chapter 1 - What is Autophagy

This chapter will deal with the definition, the working of autophagy, the types of autophagy and the usage of autophagy in the coming time. This chapter will also include the various formations of autophagy through which the people's way is moved forward in the direction. The contextualization of the book is as follows:

Definition

According to Doctor Priya Khorana, the process of autophagy means the exit of food through the stomach and it makes the metabolism look very clean. The cells that are used in this process are easily removed during this process and later there is the rejuvenation of newer cells for healthy growth for the humans. Auto means self and the word phagy means eating. Therefore, autophagy means that the body will eat automatically and with the passage of time, the old food will be removed.

By some authors, it is also related to self-devouring. This is the beneficial omen for your body and the process of self-devouring, the body cells are easily extinguished from the body thoroughly. The process of cellular repair also takes place in this context and the over-all body metabolism reaches its zeal. Thus, the use of cellular repair will make the body look better in the coming. The process of autophagy is a revolutionary self-preserving mechanism that helps in the elimination of carbon-related diseases in the human body.

For some, the definition is also contextualized as the process through which the cells of the body are easily functioned in a better manner. There is also the removal of debris. It is referred to as the process of recycling and removing at the same time. The prolific medical scientist referred to it as the way of resetting your body and the body aims to reach the better part of life. It is also a promotion of better toxin-related concepts of the body and it will amplify the metabolism of the body in a perpetual manner.

Why autophagy works

There is an ancient saying that the body will work if led with a proper mind. The use of autophagy helps to instill a proper mode of management for the people through which the persons are able to lead a happy life. The working of autophagy is also productive because it is able to give marvelous and potential results to the human body. It creates the possibility and creation of better cells that are quite great in their number and they are able to curb strong measurements of disease prevention in them. There are many other benefits of it through which the body is able to receive better quality digestion and heat of hydration. There are numerous working mechanisms that are cultivated in the body through the use of autophagy. Since, the use of autophagy brings about better changes in the human body, therefore, the use of autophagy works in the coming time and it is much effective for the use of the human body.

Autophagy for health

There are five important ways through which autophagy works for the construction of health for the students and civilians. These ways help to restore the health factor for autophagy constructively.

1. Eating a high fat, low carb diet

The eating of a high-fat triggers autophagy in the body. The use of high fat and its gestation ultimately exits some cells from the body through which the people are able to have a better understanding of the body in their dimension. The low carb diet will make your suit for autophagy as the process of elimination of cells will be random in the body and the person will be able to give more value to its body. So, the intake of high fat will make the body have more leniency in it and with the passage of time, the body will get rid of all the cells that make the body look pale and obstructive in the coming time.

2. Go on a protein fast

The autophagy will be helpful for the protein fast. Because in this fast you will be able to do a lot of mass exemption from the body. During the fast of the body, the people will be able to have a better comprehension of the body through which the protein of the body will go away and the body will be given a better way of creating proteins in the coming time. Therefore, going on a protein fast will help to make the body a much better and more regulatory space.

3. Practice Intermittent Fasting

The concept of intermittent fasting is that the body has to take a lot of proteins from the human body and there is a regular break from eating and drinking. There are time intervals through which the body is able to garner more food and water in the body. This time can be used to make the body look better and productive in the coming time. The use of strong fasting can make the body relax and have a sustainable piece of working in the coming. So, if you want to attain a benefit of autophagy of health then do practice intermittent fasting.

4. Exercise Regularly

Exercising regularly can also initiate a fast rate of autophagy for you. The exercising helps to reduce fats allowing for more proteins to actually work in the body. The working of the body helps to maintain a strong pH value of the system and the body is able to foment a healthier metabolism. This is a concept through which the autophagy of the body functions in a better way and with the passage of time, autophagy tends to be sustainable in a better function.

5. Drink a lot of water

Drinking a lot of water also helps you to maintain a stable metabolism of yourself through which you are able to have a yielding understanding of things around. Drinking a lot of water makes the ph value system aware of all the things happening around and with the passage of time, the body is able to make healthier changes in the coming time. Drinking a lot of water will keep the diet clean and healthy and it will make your body fit for any changes coming in the contemporary. Therefore, drinking a lot of water is crucial for you to maintain an autophagy state.

Types of Autophagy

There are three types of autophagy. One is the macro-autophagy, micro-autophagy and chaperone-mediated autophagy.

1. Macro-autophagy

Macro-autophagy is a type of autophagy in which the degradation of organelles occurs. It is a matured vesicle process. It is strongly recommended for the homeostasis process, in which the persons belonging to various paths and parallels are identified in the human being for a perpetual state of mind. The use of macro-autophagy can be illustrated in many ways of the world. The uses are very much in use these days. The use of microautophagy can be related to many uses like the cure of brain diseases and brain coverages. The use of macroautophagy has many abilities embedded in it. It can be used to treat neurodegenerative diseases for the people. The disease-linked aggresomes can be used in many uses to make the fossils and the human platelets working in a better way. The macroautophagy can also be constructed in many ways possible for the people coming forward. Therefore, Macroautophagy is the branch of autophagy, which deals with the process of clearing the established fats in the body.

2. Micro-autophagy

The construct of microautophagy is different from two types of autophagy that are macro and chaperone-mediated autophagy. These autophagias help the micro people and the lysosomal action to be easily overridden by the people and the body state. This practice is adopted by many people abroad and it can also be found with many people and other doctors to be precisely relevant. This practice is very important for the functioning of cells and it helps to give more emphasis to the extermination of diseases in the coming time. Cytoplasmic material is trapped in the cells of the people and the people are able to manifest the uses of autophagy properly. This process is also used for nitrogen deprivation and it can lead to strong illustrations of people effectively. There are three special cases to microautophagy. Micro hexalogy, piecemeal microautophagy and microautophagy of the nucleus. These phages make the body of the human being emerged from the ashes.

There are very important functions of micro-autophagy. There are used for nutrient recycling. This is done for the degradation of lipids. It regulates the composition of the vacuolar membrane. There are many mechanisms of glycogen in it. The pathway that comes through micro-autophagy helps to create a link with the multivesicular bodies, endocytic, membrane proteins and the use of strong organelle size. There is also non-selective micro-autophagy in this regard. There is membrane invagination, vesicle formation, vesicle expansion, vesicle degradation and selective micro-autophagy. These invaginations help to create a better formation of body cells for the persons coming forward and with the passage of time, the body is able to eat all the fats and vitamins of the structure effectively. This practice is of strong use and pertinence and can be regarded effectively in the coming time.

The process of selective micro-autophagy can be observed in all types of eukaryotic cells. This on the other hand is also commonly observed in yeast cells. Therefore, micro-autophagy helps to create a cluster of better engines for the coming community.

3. Chaperone-mediated autophagy

This chaperone-mediated autophagy helps to give more ideas to the process of autophagy. This is referring to the selection of chaperone dependent selection. The selection of soluble proteins is taken in this account. The cytosolic proteins are targeted to lysosomes and directly are related to the concept of lysosome membrane without the requirement of the formation of additional values. The proteins that want to make the structure of CMA are cytosolic proteins and proteins from other compartments. There are some compartments that discuss the nature of CMA and they are worthy to be discussed here. These are the compartments that tend to make the working of the cells more functional and linear in their working. There is selectivity of proteins and the proteins are able to make the manufacture of the engine more compatible. The CMA can be of many uses and regards of the people and the people are able to blend with the work coherently.

The proteins that participate in the CMA are more likely to be engulfed by the main cell of the body. First there is the degradation of cells, there is the presence of cytosolic protein in the making, there is the formation of amino acid in the work, there is lysosome-associated work of the protein type A in the formation, there is a receptor for the membrane of the formation of the work, the two isoforms are found in the cells of the body through which one has to trade genes to the people coming ahead, there are substrates that deal with the process of working for the people and then there are translocation purposes that make the deal of CMA more workable. There is an artificial use of people that do not cater properly to the formation of the work and with the passage of time, there is a better comprehension thing coming forward.

The matter comes to the people of the formation in a close manner and this thing helps to bind the CMA more effectively for the people. Therefore, the use of a close manner can be sorted out more periodically in the coming time. There are some limitations to the CMA process. One is the binding of the substrate of the people coming forward and with the passage of time, the CMA tends to be more linear with time. There are some levels of constraints to the process of CMA as well. With the passage of time, the CMA tends to devolve and if one wants to maintain a proper outlook of CMA then there need to be some limitations. The levels of CMA are easily utilized and they are made under some uncertainties for the people. The people in these uncertainties are not able to proceed with CMA and hence, they are able to come stringently ahead.

These are three types of autophagias discussed above in the effective manner.

Chapter 2 - 9 reasons why autophagy is good for health

This chapter will deal with this discussion about why autophagy is good for health.

1. Autophagy saves your life

As the definition of autophagy has been established above that it is the science in which the body eats its own food so this process can easily save your life effectively. In this process, the eating of fat clearly eliminates the bad food and process that could be hard to tackle while working and with the passage of time, autophagy can bring forth more progress to the people. The autophagy regularities are very effective to handle and they give an enriched benefit while the food is being conserved or stored and with the passage of time, the people are able to learn the advantages of autophagy ultimately.

2. Autophagy improves the length and quality of life

How autophagy improves the length and quality of life, this is a certain assertion needs to be answered. The autophagy people are the people that are confident with their lifestyles, they know what to eat and how to present themselves in front of others and how the improvement is able to be fostered in the coming time. Their body metabolisms make the personality of life much better and they are quite sturdy in their workings coming forward. Therefore, autophagy is able to bolster the length and quality of life in the coming time.

3. Autophagy helps your metabolism work better

The thing about autophagy that cherishes the most is its ability to make the workings better and coherent. The use of autophagy can make the body very lean and effective in its domain and with the passage of time, the people are able to have muscular bodies through it. The metabolism also functions better because of a caring appetite, autophagy has to offer. This caring appetite makes the body completely firm to come forward and with the passage of time, the people are able to have a better relaxation of the time. So, with such benefits, autophagy helps your metabolism to work better.

4. Autophagy helps you to clear out neurodegenerative diseases

The brain is the vibrating and the most important muscle of the body as it governs messages and neutronic transmissions throughout the body. If there are neurodegenerative diseases in the brain and the brain is not able to make proper processions in the body then with the passage of time, the body is able to vacate the diseases effectively. The crux of autophagy is defined to make the brain more adaptable and managerial with the passage of time and thus, the human brain is not able to make any impulsion whatsoever in the coming time. Therefore, autophagy helps you to clear out neurodegenerative diseases.

5. Autophagy helps to regulate inflammation

The process of autophagy is also essential while maintaining a level of inflammation in the body. The process is all found in the founding of the body through which the body reduces the risk of noises in the coming. The inflammation is the increase in blood pressure and with a special piece of autophagy fast forward, the people are able to make things more effective for their bodies. This is the autophagy that one needs to understand in the coming and the inflammation is all pertinent for the body to come. Therefore, autophagy is much useful for inflammation to come in line.

6. Autophagy helps us find infectious diseases regularly

Autophagy is also very effective when it comes to fighting infectious diseases. The body engine is designed in such a length through which the body is able to make devoid of things effectively. The infectious diseases that make the bodies more workable will be used in this regard. The autophagy will make the body length much lean and cooperative and with the passage of time, the body is able to nurture effectively in the coming. Therefore, autophagy is more complacent for you when it comes to fight infectious diseases regularly.

7. Autophagy also improves muscle performance

How muscle performance is improved this needs to be discussed here in detail. Muscles are used to make more time in the coming and they are built on certain vascular tissues that are round in their shape. Muscles get rusted if there is no proper use of a keto diet and proper intake of carbo related diet in the muscles and with the passage of time, the muscles need to be in a better linear order than before. So, the use of autophagy is also helpful in making muscle performance more compatible and lenient in its design.

8. Autophagy helps prevent cancer loss

Autophagy helps to control cancer brewing in the human body. It prevents cancer from further burgeoning in the human body and with the passage of time, the human body is able to supplement strong things compatibly. It can also control genome stability and can improve the working DNA more coherently. The risk of cancer is easily controllable when it comes to the induction of autophagy in it. The research process will be highly appreciable for the coming tasks of the world and the people will be able to apply with the passage of time. The crux of autophagy will help the patients to come evolving with time and the people will learn things more compatibly and ferociously.

9. Autophagy improves digestion health

The process of autophagy is very material for the use of health. It helps to give better stamina, stable mental systems and the use of effective neutronic systems that can make the body immune to diseases. It can lower the ph value with a possible rate of affection and with the passage of time, the community is able to learn things in a much better and compatible manner. The platform of autophagy can further nourish many creative aesthetics for the body and so with the passage of time, the body will be able to improve health systematically.

10. Autophagy improves your skin health

Once you are eating things in an effective manner, you are actually making a better overview of your skin effectively. The idea here is very simple, that is you have to come up with splendid assertions that can make the body look more effective in the coming. The skin gets all right and great with the passage of time and you are able to witness the portfolio of yourself holistically. Therefore, the process of autophagy is very resourceful for the public and the people can learn a lot for the coming time.

11. Autophagy may support a healthy weight

Autophagy requires a fat eating process. The fats, lipids and proteins all are very healthy for the coming time and with the process of time, autophagy is able to inculcate a better process of stamina building in you. The use of strong weight and proper digestion helps you to make things turn around in a systematic manner and with the passage of time, your muscles become rigid and you become more and more reflective in their time.

12. Autophagy minimizes self-death of cells

The regeneration of cells is an important aspect through which people are able to form multiple dimensions in the coming time. The edifice of autophagy helps to minimize the death of cells in the human being and the people are able to create better understandings of their body respectively. Therefore, the minimization of dead cells is found using autophagy.

Chapter 3 - How Autophagy works

This chapter will talk about the working of autophagy that how it comes with respect to time.

The basics

Autophagy has described above is a self-digesting mechanism of the human body. It involves the formation of a double-membrane vesicle through which the individual is able to see the fats of the body go in depletion. This process is also used to add the encapsulation of cytoplasm and other materials in an evolving manner with the passage of time. There are sixteen level autophagy protein involved in this manner. These systems produce modified complexes of autophagy regulators. There is the process of nucleation and completion of autophagias formation and then it is used to fuse it with lysosomes. There are two processes that are required in this scenario and with the passage of time, the people are able to make huge benefits through it. In mammals there are proteins that tend to deal with it.

The elongation also occurs in the process of autophagy where the people are able to have a better version of things coming with the passage of time. There is a kinase activity that is required in this process through which the individuals are harbor better credentials of the things required in the process. Atg 13, Atg 1 and Atg 2 were easily associated with the remark. All these autophagy proteins require the formation of many other instruments in a proper fashion in this regard. The elongation has the combination of two ubiquitin conjugation materials in this regard. It remains bound to the autophagosome membrane until some of it is easily bonded to the membrane. As soon as autophagous formation is completed, the Atg 16, Atg 32 and Atg 5 are there to recognize things in an appropriate manner. Now the completed autophagosome is ready for fusion with the end of the molecules and with the passage of time, the people are able to have a better understanding of the process.

The process of autophagy regulation is adamant to make the metabolism of the body more adaptable and the basics are enough for the body to undergo a positive change in themselves.

Insulin also regulates autophagy in the human body. These moments of autophagy will always be up to the mark of other people coming forward and the people, who come under the pressure of bad working as an insult so therefore, it is necessary to understand that how the formation of autophagy comes forward and it can come with many possible directions in the coming.

Mutations of many other autophagy-related ingredients for the prospect of better metabolism and health factor. There is a damage regulated autophagy modulator that tries to deal with the assertion of making the fats level descend with the passage of time. There is a manner in which the death level of the organisms is raised to death and the cell organisms are able to make the people go with positive sway. The p 53 committed cell membrane helps to make body level very mature with the passage of time and the people are able to induce much more betterment in the body. There is chromatin remodeling and the persons are able to induce more and more enrichments with the passage of time.

Macroautophagy

This is a type of autophagy. The autophagy will give immense pleasure to the cell bodies that are functioning well in the body. This is the type of autophagy that will give a clear perception of things coming in the letdown process and it kills the process of cell destruction easily. This is autophagy, which usually gives many deprivations to the body but with the passage of time, it evolves the body to a stable state.

Micro-autophagy

This autophagy involves the use of cellular disintegration which can be very healthy for the human body.

Chaperone mediated autophagy

This is the evolved process of autophagy and macro-autophagy.

Other types of autophagy

As per scientific evidence, there is no other use of autophagy required to illustrate. But there is more emphasis to bone autophagy

Autophagy used in other therapeutic agents

Autophagy is used in therapeutic agents to cure neurogenic agents.

Chapter 4 - Stimulating autophagy

In this chapter the stimulation of autophagy will be approached.

Fasting

Fasting needs to be done in order to observe the advantages of autophagy. Following meat plans need to be followed.

1. Black and white Pudding

This pudding has a fixed amount of cream in it that is used as a dessert in all the foods and can be re-created on many festivals and food. It is organic in its nature and can be created in a very short span of time. It is very fresh and a lot of customers want to have a taste of it once they have done eating their regular meals.

2. Ginger Bread Biscuits

Gingerbread biscuits are widely celebrated in all parts of the world and they are eaten with full relish as well. These biscuits are very keen on their core as they tend to be very fresh and are consumed on a daily amount of basis. The gingerbread biscuits are present in all prices and ranges for the customers that want to eat it. They are affordable in their limits.

3.   Liquor Chocolates

Liquor chocolates are very delicious and they have a taste of liquor in them, which adds a taste of acidity in them. The amount of liquor is very fresh for the body as it easily gives a fresh tone of digestion to the body. There is less heat generated in the body while drinking it and it can be very helpful at times for many festivals. It is important to have a healthy diet these days and if liquor chocolates are used as a means to get to the balanced chart then they must utilize it at all costs.

4.   Chicken made with a stuffing of fruits and vegetables

Chicken, which is made with a lot of acidic strains, if it is combined with a stuffing of fruits and vegetables; then it can be very ketogenic for the consumers. The process is very healthy for the people and it ensures all the strong amounts of protein intake that humans can vitalize. This is the ability of chicken mixed with vegetables that can be very helpful for the individuals.

5.   Haggis

It is a stomach of sheep, which is embedded with oatmeal and offal. This oatmeal and offal can be very effective for the metabolism of the individuals as it produces a great range of intakes for the people. There is a residue of acidic strains and ketogenic inputs that give the customer a relishing tone to digest. It is made with proper care and intellect and can be further assessed for many benefits. It is not only available in Scotland but can be retrieved also in other countries. This is a better provision for the customers, which gives it proper digestion and intake.

6. Dumpling Soup

The dumpling soup is revered by the doctors to be very helpful at the present age. A lot of people whether living in the west or the east are consuming a lot of amount of ketogenic and acidic diet for their daily usage. This intake creates an acidic heat in the body and in this way the dumpling soup caters to this dilemma with full urge and discipline. What happens is that the moment the soup is entrained into the windpipe of the human; the body system becomes very energetic. Hence, the dumpling soup is able to get a lot of help for the human body and it is also recommended by many.

7. Toshikoshi Soba

Toshikoshi Soba is a Japanese dish that can easily deal with the autophagy of the body. It is baked using a ketogenic powder that can be very helpful for the consumers. It has a spread of noodles all around it that can give an acidic taste as well. It is for all the consumers and individuals that want a balanced diet in their bodies and it can turn around to be very effective and helpful to the local people. It is affordable by a layman throughout Japan and it has fresh ingredients that are recommended for the body.

8.   Latkes

If you want a ketogenic diet that has fresh vegetables and juices, then you must refer to latkes. It is an Israeli diet that has all the fresh ingredients that your body can use and you can come up with a healthy amount of taste for it. All you need is to develop a mindset in your body that you want to achieve the best of you. There are crispy potato chips engraved in it and there can be more possibilities in it as well. You can have the entire taste and relish of it. Just buy it near any store and you will achieve the best of your health as well.

9.   Puerto Rican Pasteles

Puerto Rican Pasteles is the famous dish that is available in Puerto Rico and it can be very fresh for the public over there. It is made with raisins, olives, pork, and fish. The tamales that are made are frozen first and then they are served to their customers. The reason for their freezing is because they can be well served while they are frozen. The pastels are also very affordable for all the customers located in various parts of the world and there are many special features of them. They can be curated in all sizes and demands.

10.   Carmela

If you are a vegetarian and are avoiding chicken meats to be all lean and ketogenic then this cabbage-made dish is the real deal for you. You have to be very cautious while eating as its single intake can be very heavy.

Not only cabbage but it has a slight amount of chicken ginger folds that can be very helpful for digestion. Therefore, it is important to have a balanced diet on holiday and this diet is recommended by all the prodigies to be of supreme relish.

11. Jansson's Temptation

This dish is very delicious and it starts with a tempting scotch of potato casserole and cream herring. This temptation compels the customer to it and there are many positive reviews about it in the country. Family and middle-class men all are enjoying it and they require a lot of usage for it. Also, this dish comes in all prices and ranges and there are many varieties to it as well.

12. Carp

This carp has a special amount of green leaves decorated at its sides and it can be used to access the food regime of human metabolism. The autophagy that is produced by this dish is very instrumental in its making and it provides all the comfort levels that can be used to get a hydrated amount of autophagy in it. The carp creates a sense of relish in the human body and due to it; it allows the person to grow more diet tactics. You can easily be healthy and fresh throughout your routine.

13. Mince Pie

This dish of England has its own taste to check and one can easily afford the autophagy in his body through it. The diet of the human body is very important to be maintained on holidays and this mince pie can be the real deal for the humans. The mince pie has a sweet touch to it that makes the customer very happy about it.

14. Yebeg Wot

This is a Christmas dish that has a very good reputation worldwide. It is created by giving a soft lamb pouring all around it. This Wot is spread with flatbread and it can be very helpful for the eaters to have fun for it.

15. Tamales

These tamales are portable corn husk rolls that can be very instrumental for the diet appetite. These are present in all names and sizes and can be effective in all ins and outs. They are presentable in all fruits, vegetables, and cheeses.

16. Mashed Potatoes

The last recipe to this list is mashed potatoes. These potatoes are very instrumental in their making and they have to be boiled and peeled to see how they are formed. They are mashed in a proper way to attract the customers and they have an attractive lure all around them.

Therefore, these are the food and diets that can be used to celebrate in different parts of the world. They are celebrated and adored all around the world. People come from all the places to see the attraction, the taste and the uniqueness of these dishes. They are used to induce autophagy in the human body.

While fasting following foods needs to be avoided at all costs.

1.   Sugary Drinks

Sugar is a dangerous product and a demanding food recipe. It can be sweet and at the same time, it can require a lot of sweat to be removed from the body. All those drinks like the Pepsi drinks and the hydrated drinks that have an amount of sugar in them are too difficult to be removed from the day that the human body has to do a lot of grueling exercise for them. Also, the blood vessels that get in contact with the sugar streamline are two exposed to collapse because these sugar particles tend to disturb the vessels of the human body. Furthermore, the sugary drinks also disturb the healthy metabolism of the body and also they make the routine of the body very lazy. Therefore, the sugary drinks need to be avoided at all cost to stay healthy and fit.

2.   Pizzas

Pizzas carry a lot of calorie and chemical products that are able to make you fat and lazy. These pizzas always create a source of relish for the individuals but nobody knows what happens in the latter. Pizzas have to be eaten but there needs to be a systematic kind of balance while they are being consumed. The dairy products, the cheese, and the bread all are able to create a lot of fat tendencies among the individuals that eat it. Thus, it is mandatory for people to realize the plight of this fast food. Otherwise, it can be very detrimental to the public.

3.   White Bread

Although white bread is considered to be very healthy for the individuals in the morning; but it also has some detrimental qualities as well. White bread contains a vicious amount of calories that can raise the blood level of humans. It is also the real reason behind the vast emergence of heart strokes in the patients. Therefore, it is important to take a minimum amount of bread in the morning. Also, there is an alternative to this dairy product as well. The brown bread can be used as an alternative as it carries a lesser amount of calories in it.

4.   Industrial Vegetable Oils

Industrial vegetable oils are very acidic in nature. They carry a lot of calories, fat oils and other dairy ingredients in them. There are also added fats in them that tend to create a lot of hurdles for body metabolism. Their intake can create troubles in blood clotting and it can also be the reason for heart attacks. Industrial vegetable oils are very precarious for health. They all can be very haunting for the consumers; there needs to be minimum use of vegetable oils for cooking recipes.

5. Margarine

Margarine is presumed to be like butter but it has many cancerous ingredients to it. Margarine possesses all the important components of butter like amino acids, fats, and lipids, which can cause a urinary impact on the body. It is, therefore, very important that the use of margarine be minimized at all costs. The alternative to this product can be the use of butter as it has minimum calories in it.

6. Pastries, cookies, and cakes

We all like to eat a lot of pastries and cookies because we get attracted to their odor and taste. They have the variety that qualifies for our interest and we like to stuff our bellies with a lot of pastries just for the moment of fun. However, we do not know that these cakes and pastries have calorie content that is very enjoyable for us. But fewer people know that they create stubborn fat in our bellies that require a lot of effort and exercise to let it go. Also, they are the primary reason for a lazy routine and if their consumption is kept forward then they will reduce the ketogenic process of the body.

7. French Fries.

If you think that you want to obese in a short span or want to win a fat body competition, then potato fries and French fries are the real deal for you. Without their intake, you cannot be fat. Although this statement donates a connotation that the fries are good but their storage can lead to the rise of many inflammatory diseases in the human body. They also have a profuse amount of calorie intake in their body and thus, can make you look lazy. The acidity in your body can rise to its acme if the accumulation of French fries is taken in your body.

8. Agave Nectar

Agave nectar contains a large amount of fructose in the body that can yield a lot of sweetness in your blood. This sweetness can compact your vessels and make your metabolism become dull and void. Also, kidney fractures and other bodily malfunctions come in your body and you can get the worst amount of digestion in no time. So the intake of agave nectar is not good for your body and you must try your best in making the less of it.

9. Low Fat Yogurt

Yogurt is a healthy product, which is very supplementary for your health. It has a relevant of dairy ingredients that boost activeness and agility in you. You get a fresh start to your routine if you are able to muster up usage. There is a minimum amount of fat stored in it as well. However, low-fat yogurt is not good as it contains an obsess amount of yogurt that could be detrimental for you. It has profuse lipids that can make your face look pale in no time and it can be also quite dangerous to store in the belly. Instead of it, one should go for the full-fat yogurt that has good calorie content for you and you can feel all fresh and great for it. The low-fat yogurt can be put to the fermentation process and its fermentation can yield an enormous amount of protein for you.

10. Ice cream

Ice cream is used as a dessert for many but it has a great number of calories stored in it. It comes in all flavors and like the other acidic foods mentioned above, it can lead to proper storage of fats in your body. Also, the biscuit content that is present below the ice-cream has a huge number of calories in it and thus, the ice cream is a fat creating package for you. You can make a great alternative to this menace by creating better ice cream. For creating the better version of ice cream, mature ingredients need to be used for better results.

11. Candy Bars

If you want to carry a short snack with you that can create a fatty metabolism in you, then candy bars are the real menace to be blamed. Created with a touch of candy, flavored with sugar and coated with chocolates; these ingredients reflect the highest amount of acidity in your body. They boost calorie content in you. They create fat storages in you and they do not let to go away in a jiffy. They have a lot of bars of accumulation in their creation and they all are very haunting for you. Thus, it is important that candy bars are pertinent to be stayed away from and their intake can damage your cholesterol level as well.

12. Processed Meat

Meat is the highest amount of protein giver than any other food. However, processes meat needs to be finished by all means possible. Because it has all the chemical ingredients that trigger fat accumulation in your body and it is very dampening for human metabolism as well. It is also not covered in healthy packing and it gives a sheer amount of negativity in your body as well. The meat further destroys the good quality of chlorine in your body and you are not able to regain the advantages of a balanced diet in a sensible way.

13.   Processed Cheese

Processed cheese is filled with filler ingredients that completely eradicate protein and healthy fats in your body. On the contrary, regular cheese is very fine for the body as the content of food is compatible with your body. Therefore, the idea of processed cheese is not good for your body as it destroys the healthy metabolism of the body.

14.   Veggie Petties

Veggie Petties are very good for health but their procession can also be very daunting for the human body. The vegetables that are used in these sandwiches have a chlorine-deficit in it and can not be used as a healthy regimen. Because chlorine impacts your blood and having a chlorine-deficit diet can make you feel tired and can boost you in becoming a lazy person. Also, it can accumulate a vast amount of fats in the body. You are not able to feel fresh when you eat a lot of veggie patties. You are not able to get the quality of intake of freshness in the body and thus, you end up being fat and there is a massive increase of cholesterol in the body.

15.   Packaged Turkey

Turkey has an abundance of sodium and proteins in it but a package of it is not able to give the amount of balanced diet that you want. Its packaging is very detrimental for your level and you end up becoming very unhygienic throughout the year. You can either buy less sodium in the package or you will end up being lazy and feel very unhealthy. Thus, packaged turkey is a good diet but not a ketogenic diet to eat.

16.   Energy Bars

These energy bars are hailed to be energy bars but you are not able to achieve an energy full diet because of it. The energy bars are not able to give an important intake of proteins as well. According to Dr. Garwis, protein bars are all just processed chemicals. And also, they have a lot of chemicals embedded in them. They are chemical creators that do not give enough health to the individuals and they are able to a sustained metabolism rate for the individuals.

17.   Bran Muffins

This recipe can be a quick breakfast diet but actually, it leaves a lot of calories especially for the individuals, who consume it. It has a profuse chemical of sugar, formaldehyde, wheat, and flour and they all try their best to creating fats in themselves.

18. Multigrain Bread

This bread has the sugar embedded chemical in it that can be harmful to your body if taken massively. It is assumed to be very healthy as it has a multi-grain fiber attached to it but overall, it required a lot of wheat and sugar in it, which can be detrimental for you. It can also spike the blood sugar level in you and you will feel remorseful while you are eating it.

19. Flavored Oatmeal

Well, do you think that you can find any faults in regular oatmeal when it is served in front of you; because it has everything that the body required? However, research is proved that oatmeal tends to boost massive calories in you as it has a lot of sodium and sugar-related chemicals staked in it. Also, the creamy flavor fosters fats and chemicals in yourself and can be very dangerous for you as well.

20. Reduced-Fat Peanut Butter

The reduced-fat peanut butter is very good for breakfast or even regular lunch meals. It has a reduced amount of sodium intake in it and contains fewer fats comparatively. They are naturally created with the fermentation process of the sugar. However, they have one strong drawback. That is that they have to be energy deficit and they can bring more fats in the bodies due to reduced-fat peanut butter.

21. Couscous

Couscous might be a vital grain to feast but it is just like pasta because it is very dangerous in its making. Couscous want to build the massive intake of autophagy in you and you want it for any reason. However, the sugar and sodium level in couscous is very high and at some level, it can be very dangerous for you as well.

Therefore, these foods are not good for the body intake as they dampen the healthy figments of the body and try to impede positive metabolism in the body. The damage that these ingredients due to their bodies are very obscene and there must be the use of super-foods that can heal the body with full zeal.

So, in fasting the aforementioned foods need to be avoided and used accordingly.

Dieting

While dieting, do your best to make the best out of you and eat the following foods.

1. Kelp

Kelp is a portion of fresh green food that boosts iodine intake in the body. It is also rich in calcium, magnesium, and potassium, which can be very supplemental for the body. The intake of kelp should be very moderate to give the body a nominal control of its care. The green ingredients reduce fat and terrible amino acids that could be harmful to the body. Also, the love handles that are created on the sides of the stomach are easily rectified with full zeal and energy.

2. Ginger

Ginger is very useful in treating arthritis and can very suitable for healthy digestion as well. It is recognized worldwide for its ability to treat nausea and it has been doing it in a spectacular way.

3. Mushrooms

There are many types of mushrooms that can cater to healthy digestion in the body. The types include a white button, shiitake, portabella, and cremini. These mushrooms also lower the cholesterol level in the body and create a ketogenic state of digestion in the human body. These mushrooms are easy to cook and eat and apart from healing benefits, they can be used in desserts as well.

4. Beets

Beets contain a plethora of many supplements for the body. They give carbs, calcium, iron, vitamin a and vitamin c. These vitamins are very helpful for the body as they regenerate a lot of energy for the body to do work. Many people in the contemporary world are pursuing beets for the gain of carbohydrates. Beets are easy to buy and afford and can be able to give outstanding performances in the human body.

5. Probiotics

First, let us understand what are probiotics? Probiotics are the microorganisms that attack germs entering your body and they are very useful in making you aloof of diseases. They are very tiny in their chemistry that can be found in yogurt, kefir and soy beverages.

These probiotics can also be obtained in many other products as well. These probiotics can be used to treat irritable bowel syndrome, skin infections, and certain cancers.

6.   Swiss Chard

This chard provides a huge amount of source for vitamins c,e, and k for the human body. It also gives fiber, zinc, and calcium. The chard is also available in a variety of leaf colors. The taste is the combination of salty and bitter. This nutrition-packed vegetable must be supporting bone health; fights stress-related disease and also have the anti-inflammatory disease to cater as well.

7.   Aloe Vera

Aloe Vera is a curing herb that is used to heal facial scars and also cater to the digestion burns in the body. The digestion that is due to an acidic diet creates burning conditions in the body and the intake of aloe vera can also provide healthy minerals for the body. It is found in almost every price and variation. It has an anti-inflammatory nature in it and it attacks all the inflammatory diseases that can be precarious for the body. A bio-mediating form is also present in the core of Aloe Vera that tries to provide better compensation for the results in a human body. Also, this herb specialized in curing the headache of the body and tries its best to create a moderate form in the body. Aloe vera has all the proper chemical ingredients that can create sustenance of the entire human system. Therefore, aloe vera is a healthy herb that is very helpful for the body to heal.

There are many spiritual lessons apparent in Aloe Vera as well. Coming from healing, herb relaxes the system of the mental coordination of a human body and the human being, who is taking the herb comes into an emotional connection with the herb. The herb transcends its healing qualities to humans at all cost and there is no hurdle of its extraction.

8.   Apple Cider Vinegar

Apple Cider Vinegar is a curing herb that gives all the relaxation to the human body. It is very efficient in pro-biotics that can cure the mindset of the tensed human body and it can also yield proper salvation to the human body as well. This Apple Cider is usually not found in any other product rather than green herbs and it has many other probiotics that yield safety for the humans.

9.   Lemons

Lemons are very healthy for the human metabolism. It has enriched zinc components in it that carve a spectacular body in the human structure. The digestion becomes very easy and no reverting into the esophagus is done in such a scenario. Therefore, the intake of lemons can be very helpful for the human body to enjoy and it is a total package for the human body to enjoy. Also, throat scratches and burns can be easily healed using the lemonade, which yet again is the component of lemon.

Exercising

For exercising, you have to do regular physical exercise along with minute level weight training.

Chapter 5 - Water fasting and ketosis diet

Water fasting and ketosis diet helps to maintain a better place of autophagy in your body. The meals required for water fasting are as follows:

Extended Water fasting

1. Tomatoes

Tomatoes are the best ketogenic foods one can possibly have. It has many nutrients in it. Tomatoes are a great source of Vitamin c. They also provide Vitamin B6. You can have a tomato and then can use it in your favorite salad as well. Therefore, it is an enriched supplement that provides you a ketogenic diet.

2. Almonds

If you want to have a quick ketogenic supplement, then an almond can serve the best purpose to you. They are composed of high fats and can be easily used to store a good amount of energy in you. Also, there is no grueling amount of energy required while its consumption.

3. Spinach

The leafy vegetable, which is green in color is very good for health. It is also very versatile in nature. Spinach can yield the best amount of taste for the public as it verily recommended by all the medical experts. If you want a fresh ketogenic breakfast, then spinach is the real deal for you.

4. Parsley

Parsley is a ketogenic food that is rich in autophagy. It can be used for various purposes as well. It can be used to cleanse the kidney level and can be used in curbing heat digestion. You can also use its variety in many ways to make your food look good.

5. Jalapeno

For a healthy ketogenic diet, the jalapeno is very crucial for health. Jalapeno can be used in many ways and tactics to get to know the autophagy of the body. This ketogenic supplement can support the endocrine system as well.

6. Avocado

If you are a bodybuilder and want to assume yourself to be the next big thing in the world then you surely have to try avocado. This supplement is the powerhouse for you. If you use it properly then certainly you can achieve all the healthiness and agility, you want in your body.

7. Basil

Basil is an amazing ketogenic supplement that is designed to boost energy in your bodies. It is composed of a scientific chain of carbohydrates that ensures anti-inflammation in your body. It is available in all pieces and products anywhere in the shop. It is very quick to eat and it has all the products to be ensured. Therefore, it is important for the supplements to be taken properly and in order to be ketogenic in nature, the supplement basil can be arranged systematically.

8. Dark Lettuces

If you are missing the fantastic dark lettuces for your ketogenic diet then you are committing the worst blunder of your life. You have to try this ingredient as it will enormous health benefits and the only way you are able to reap its benefits is that you understand its mechanism at all costs. It has a deep color of minerals in it. The color indicates special vitamins for your body like vitamin c and vitamin k. The green pigment includes chlorophyll in your body and you can end up being very fresh in your daily routine.

9. Celery

This is a great alkalizing food for many reasons. It has a huge amount of water in it. It has vitamins like c and k. The composition is filled with electrolytes that can provide health to your body in no time. This ketogenic also reduces high blood pressure. This food can be easily chopped and diced anywhere and can be presentable in all forms and sizes. The cream of celery is also very great for you in all regards.

10.   Carrots

Carrot is a favorite ketogenic food for many. IT has all the potential vitamins in it that can be used with full zeal and glory. Vitamins like A and C are present in a massive amount. You can also use them in your fruit juices like the green juice. You can also roast them in many ways possible and they can serve as an excellent model of decoration for your barbecue. However, not a lot more cooking must be there because a lot of cooking can make the food very acidic. There are sweet potatoes and orange winter squash that is used in many dishes for you. The rosemary roasted carrots, the curry-spiced carrots, and spiced carrots can be helpful in any desire or circumstance.

11. Sea Vegetables

Sea vegetable serves as excellent recipes and supplements when you want to serve yourself with autophagy . It is rich in magnesium, calcium, and sodium. It is embedded with vitamins. Vitamins like A, C and K. They are basically eaten in a macrobiotic diet for this purpose. Sea veggies are also popular to have an ocean-like flavor, though they make tasty additions and salads as well. Nori wraps are a very excellent replacement for grain-based wraps.

12. Sprouted Almonds

Almonds are a great choice for alkalizing and they need a proper mechanism to be used properly. The soaking and sprouting even have many benefits. It has many vitamins like E and C. Almonds are great vegan protein and fiber also. If you use these sprouted almonds in a homogeneous mixture then these provide anti-inflammation in no time.

13. Bok Choy

This healthy diet is capable of transforming many diets for your body. This bok choy is packed with vitamin k and c. It is very rich in antioxidants and is very cancerous for other persons as well. You can add these bok choys to soups and can give more salads and wraps in it as well. There is a simple baby bok choy, sweet and spicy bok choy, and Korean bok choy.

14. Raw Pumpkin Seeds

This beautiful supplement can be very effective for the health regime. These seeds leave ketogenic ash in the blood when they are eaten in the body. They make the body more ketogenic and purer when they are in the body and hence, these are raw in their desires as well. They have a high amount of chlorophyll in their pigments due to which the circulation of the human body is more agile and fast. They are also a great source of iron and protein. They also make a sweet crunch for your desserts as well.

15. Pink Sea Salt

The Himalayan salt has a very spree of benefits for its consumers. This salt has over eighty-four percent of minerals like magnesium, potassium, and calcium. This salt can cure headaches, joint pain, and fatigue and muscle issues. If you know what to do with the salt then you can easily buy and purchase it. You just need to consume it raw and then you can reap all the benefits of it.

16. Matcha Green Tea

The green tea is not like the regular green tea it has a great amount of nutrition for you. It is not heated or processed like any other tea and if you are able to think of other raw food then this is the prime tea. This tea has an abundance of chlorophyll in it and it has many bodily effects as well. It can improve mood and contains less caffeine for you and other acidic ingredients in it. It also has a great amount of calming effect on your body. If you want to start a great amount of breakfast in your day then this matcha green tea is the next big thing for you.

17. Spirulina

You want to have sea algae that can be very fantastic for your blood flow and if you are searching for such then spirulina is the next big thing for you. The nutrition of this diet is very healthy for your body. IT has, in it, four grams of protein that can be very captivating for your body. It is also packed with vitamin A and can give you a lot of other minerals as well.

There is no hectic amount of researching for it and you have to be very decent while searching for it. You can try it other smoothies as well. You may try it in Raspberry and Blue Spirulina Smoothie. Therefore, these kinds of diets can give you a lot of energy and relish in you for a quality of relaxation in it. Spirulina is also affected by a large amount of spiritualization that can very impact-full in this scenario.

Thus, these are the alkalizing supplements that provide enriched healthy metabolic systems to the bodies and the bodies grow exactly in all sizes and forms due to these. The supplements are carefully examined and they are attained in all costs and packages for the consumers. They generate a high rate of water fasting in you.

Ketogenic diet

The Ketogenic diet and how it works

Are you fat and looking for a planned diet to be lean and fit? Does your corporate lifestyle impede you're eating habits and does not make you feel fresh or energetic? Or simply you do not have the time to research for a balanced diet? If any of these questions bother you then I believe that you are reading the right book at the moment. This book believes in the quality of the diet and prioritizes it over-exercise. The ketogenic diet is the real answer, your obscene mind is looking for and if you apply it then yes, the big tummy of yours will be easily overridden.

The ketogenic diet has natural working. It is composed of such fruits and products that have a ketogenic PH value. This value minimizes the presence of fat and dairy products and allows you to stay healthy throughout your routine. Before, we delve what is the ketogenic diet? Let us examine what is meant by the ketogenic diet. The ketogenic diet is the diet, which has a chemical composition of fruits that have a PH value of above 7 and they are generally water-based in their chemicals. Meaning is that they have enriched quantities of hydrogen and oxygen items in them that become very sustainable for the human body to function. The ketogenic diet fruits contain oranges, mangoes, tomatoes, seeds, legumes, and tofu. In case of a heavy diet and hectic routine, we humans always want to be lean and active and if we fill our stomachs with fast food then we cannot be proactive. Hence, we need a diet that is aloof of all these fats and lipids and can sustain a healthy metabolism throughout our routine.

The working of the ketogenic diet is very progressive in its nature. It is composed of a ketogenic diet regime, which has the theory about it. The theory states that the food molecules, in a ketogenic diet, can be so pure in their PH core that they can prevent harmful diseases from occurring to the human body. This book will not delve into such controversies but would advocate the proper use of the ketogenic diet for the betterment of the human body. So, the chemical composition of a ketogenic diet is based on acidic ash and ketogenic ash. These two components are produced through various biomechanical experiments that yield potential for the people. Ketogenic ash is produced by fruits and vegetables that are green in color and have a ketogenic PH value. The liquid that is used for the synthesis of a ketogenic diet is the residue of the citrus food and acts to give a sumptuous touch to the diet.

Once a ketogenic diet is produced, it is used by consumers to prevent their feeble bodies from the dose of attack of kidney stones and heart diseases. The fruits, once they digested, they help to make the metabolism of the body very ketogenic in a natural way. No amount of burping or fat storage is apparent after the consumption of a ketogenic diet. The diet of food saves a lot of time of consumption and erases any unnecessary fat, which is being stored in the body. In this way, the working of having a ketogenic diet is very nice and it could be able the easy way to be fit. Also, working has many advantages. First and foremost, it builds a solid muscle mass, which is able to make the body look very attractive and strong. A healthy body structure can allow the body to go away in all ifs and buts. Researchers have published their study about the ketogenic diet in the journal, named as Osteoporosis International. They state that many bodybuilders also tend to use the ketogenic diet for their own benefit. Diseases like diabetes, chronic kidney disease, and cardiovascular disease can be cured and also it is meant to cure the fractured fabric in humans resulting as an outcome of sports in humans. Therefore, the major idea of a ketogenic diet is to eat fruits and vegetables and drink lemon-lime as all these components are ketogenic in nature.

Once you have done the intake of a ketogenic diet, you will feel very fresh and great. The pigments that are present in the upper surfaced of the foods give comforting digestion in your large intestine. You are not able to feel any heat burn or issues while you are intaking the ketogenic diet and thus, in no time, you are able to come close to a balanced diet. Therefore, working of the very natural ketogenic diet, calm and clean for your body.

According to scientists, autophagy can also be achieved by creating a fixed amount of diet intakes in the body. The scientists believe that if you are able to carve out a splendid moment for your appetite then this means you are actually pursuing a ketogenic diet. Therefore, it is important to understand that a fixed amount of nutrition can be very effective for your body intake and can yield success for you in no time.

The Amazing Benefits of a ketogenic diet

Do you want to be stable in your health regime and eat fresh things simultaneously? Do you think you need to know the proper diet of your regime while working and sleeping? If you want to achieve a healthy food routine, then the ketogenic diet is the real deal for you. In the previous chapters, we had discussed the alluring notions of a ketogenic diet and now, we will look into the amazing benefits of it.

First and foremost is the sheer activeness that a person tends to achieve while he is eating a ketogenic diet. He feels healthy and looks healthy and wants to be doing a lot of things while he is having a ketogenic diet. He can think properly and can get rid of inflammatory diseases that can cause him suffering. He has a strong discipline that can be navigated in any way possible and thus, he is the next big thing for his users. Also, the longevity of life in this scenario and truly, a ketogenic diet can do a lot of wonders for the individual. Therefore, a ketogenic diet has a lot to do for the fitness and active-ness in the human body.

If you want to look green and fresh on your face, then the ketogenic diet can be very helpful in this regard. Studies show that the ketogenic diet is very popular in making a healthy face for you. The number of herbs and breakfast recipes you have for yourself, up-bring a good amount of freshness on your face as well on your skin. Thus, autophagy is very crucial for having great skin and face.

Ketogenic diet protects bone density and muscle mass. The mineral intake that you get after having a ketogenic diet can protect your bone density. The bones need certain minerals that are used to cure the excessive number of hurdles one gets while running.

The minerals are given by the ketogenic diet and you are able to get a stronger bone for life. If you are a bodybuilder and want to reap the benefits of the bone then you have to accumulate more ketogenic foods in you that can be very beneficial for you. For example, muscle mass can be secured in an acute manner if you tend to get more and more almonds and other ketogenic foods. You have to be very lenient when you are having the ketogenic diet because the benefit of a ketogenic diet like the muscle mass and the bone density will be instrumental for you. Just always look at the bright side of the diet and you will feel very productive while you do it.

In today's world, tensions are like a haunting disease that wants to remain at your back for no reason. Everywhere you go, you get a tertiary level of tension. There is the tension of graduating, the tension of succeeding in life, the tension of getting a job and the tension of whatnot. You believe that the tension can be very successive for you but in the latter, it turns out to be adverse. Scientists have claimed medical drugs for its cure but the only reasonable cure is the use of a ketogenic diet. The enzymes that you get through vegetables lower the risk of your hyper blood tension and then you can achieve all the relish of your lifestyle in no time. Also, your blood level starts to resonate with full capacity and you will feel like a superman every place you go, therefore; hypertension and tensed matters get an upper hand of resolution when you get to know the prospect of a ketogenic diet.

You are able to get a lot of chronic pains in your body due to many reasons. You get to the bottom of any problem; you solve it and end up having chronic pain in your body. Chronic pain refers to any tertiary amount of pain in your body and you are able to get to the harmfulness of it in no time. Therefore, chronic pain is the most devastating headache that you can get and the only effective cure of it is the ketogenic diet. Yes, the ketogenic diet is very important for you to maintain as the blood level minimizes when lemon or other ketogenic water is induced in the body. So, this is another benefit of a ketogenic diet and it does not matter if you are a walker, a boxer or even a corporate worker, you must have a ketogenic diet in you if you wish to give all that you crave.

Recipes in a ketogenic diet

Breakfast recipes

If you want to start afresh day in your routine, then you must be able to choose fresh breakfast recipes for yourselves. Breakfast is essential for any day, which has tons and tons of work and you remain the breakfast you eat in your day. Following are some of the fresh ketogenic breakfasts that can be productive for your day

1. French toast

This breakfast is widely shared and eaten throughout the world. French toast has all the necessary ingredients that boost energy in your bodies and the ingredients are especially ketogenic in their nature. It is easily made and it gives all the proper intake to the body chain of energies. It can be made with amalgamating pieces of bread and have a sharp linger of egg on it. French toasts are recommended by doctors to the patients, who have to fight inflammatory diseases.

2. Apple Pancakes

Apple pancakes are the great treasury for you if you strive for a ketogenic diet. This diet is recommended by the entire in all ifs and buts of life. A beautiful mixing of apples in sweat odors of a cake is essential for its making. With a cup of tea, apple pancakes are the healthiest ketogenic diet of all. Also, these pancakes are very easy to make and they can be given in all ranges of prices to the customers.

For its making, you need a half cup of flour, a half teaspoon of grounded cinnamon, an egg whisked, one-third cup full of milk, two red apples, cooking oil, blueberries and low-fat frozen yogurt. With these ingredients, the apple pancakes can be easily made and there is a lot of delicious taste attached to it.

3. Avocado Breakfast Salad

This breakfast salad can help you regain all your lost energies in you when you are sleeping. It is the Mexican salad that can help you give important details to your intake at all the possible levels of your body. Its ingredients are two tortillas, half a spoon of firm tofu, one avocado, a handful of almonds, one spoon of chili sauce, half a red onion and half a lemon. It makes is very simple as well and every layman, who wants a fast and healthy diet can use this salad for its own making.

4. Mix Sprout Salad

If you want to start your day with a tasteful ketogenic diet then mix sprout is the best salad for you. It has the proteins, vitamins, minerals and energy ounces that can be very instrumental for you. Its ingredients include fifty grams of sprouts, one cucumber, one spring onion, a handful of parsley, fresh juice of a lemon, Celtic sea salt, and black pepper. The making of it is also very fundamental for you and it gives you the best amount of energy you can possibly have.

5. Kale Chickpea Mash

This dish, with its name, sounds very tasty for you and it provides all the necessary benefits for your side. The ingredients for its make contain three tablespoons of garlic, one shallot, a bunch of kale, four hundred grams of chickpeas, two tablespoons of coconut oil and Celtic tea taste for more relish. The making of this recipe is also very easy. You just need to chop out the salad in an equal manner and add some minced garlic in olive oil. Then you have to wait till it turns golden brown and then you can add some onion and garlic. Add some chickpeas and start to cook them. Put the remaining ingredients in it and pour it in it and after proper mixing, your dish is now ready to be served.

6.   Quinoa and Apple Breakfast

This breakfast food has a great combination for it. It has the finest ingredients involved in it. The ingredients are a half cup of quinoa, one apple, half a lemon, and cinnamon. These ingredients will produce the finest ketogenic breakfast for you that will have all the healthy proteins, enzymes and vitamins for you. In order to create it, you have to cook the quinoa first, you have to add some water, you have to boil the water for fifteen minutes, grate the apple and cook for thirty seconds, sprinkle some cinnamon and add raisins for a flowery taste.

7. Cold Oats

The col oat dish is an amazing breakfast ketogenic food for you that can give you early breakfasts for good metabolism. The ingredients of this meal contain half a cup of oats, half a skimmed of meat, half a cup of yogurt, half a teaspoon of cinnamon, a banana sliced, a cup of berries and a table teaspoon of berries. The steps are very easy to understand. First and foremost is the mixing of oats, seal the mixing in a jar and put it in the refrigerator, add banana slices and berries with cinnamon in the morning and after it bake it for good use.

8. Scrambled Tofu

Let us assume that you are a corporate owner and you have to go early on your job for a good lifestyle and attention, the best breakfast that you can have is scrambled tofu. The ingredients are one union, three cloves, three tomatoes, some firm tofu, half a teaspoon of cumin, half a teaspoon of paprika, half a teaspoon of turmeric, half a cup of yeast, baby spinach and salt for taste. These ingredients are great for a tonic taste for the diet and they can enough relish to the taste as well. The steps are very crucial as well. These are dicing of the onion, mincing of the garlic, the addition of some onions in a pan, the addition of some tofu and some tomatoes, the addition of cumin, paprika, and water, stirring of water and cook, the addition of spinach and flowering of the taste as well.

9. Theplas

In the southern states of Punjab of the subcontinent, Pakistan, and India, theplas is a Gujarati diet that is very ketogenic in its formation. It has ingredients of coriander, garlic, onion, spinach, salt, soya flavor, turmeric, sesame seeds, ragi flour, and capsicum. These ingredients all fill up to be a proper breakfast diet for you and you have to do the careful making of it. The steps are the addition of some oil in a pan and the heating of it for two minutes, the addition of some onion and stirring in your golden oven, the addition of capsicum, paneer, coriander, and salt and cooking for it for two minutes. Removing of the flame and letting it cool for minutes. Further comes the division of dough, cooking helps in oil. Place stuffing on top and serve it fresh.

10.   Maple Millet Porridge

A diet filled with protein and amino acids for you. These ingredients are one cup of millet, ten cups of water, a pinch of salt, one tablespoon of cinnamon and a quarter of maple syrup, which can be very productive for the human body. The steps include the taking of a large pot and boiling water for a minute, the addition of some salt and millet, the covering of lid and reduction of heat while doing it, the addition of cinnamon and almond water, the adjusting of the thickness of the food and then dishing is ready.

Therefore, these are breakfast dishes that are ketogenic in nature. They must be eaten and highly encouraged in the daily life routine. They are very easy to eat and very nice to cook. You can have all the joys and jollies while you eat them and do not others fool you about it.

Lunch Recipes

We have carefully examined the breakfast diets for you and now, it is the time to discuss the lunch recipes for you. Ideally, for a ketogenic lunch recipe, we have the fruits and other non-dairy products that can be attributed to lunch recipes. However, there are many other lunch recipes that can be used for lunch diets. The lunch recipes are as follows:

1. Summer Salad with citrus dressing

Salads make a fantastic lunch and if you dress them with juices and sprinkle salts on them then they can make good use of the health as well. You have to do all the cutting and dressing and must try your best in getting the greenish salads for your own benefit. You can only reap benefits for yourself if you are able to amalgamate tomatoes, carrots, green-leaved, cabbage and lemons in the salad. For a salty taste, you can sprinkle some salads on the salad for your own relish. This meal is very conducive for your health and can be used in many situations while you want a lunch meal for you. You have to very keen while looking at this situation and you will get all the amazing results to your body if you have a salad for yourself.

2. Cheesy Kale Chips and Sliced Fruit

These kips contain all the necessary amount of minerals, amino acids, proteins, and enzymes the human body needs. They are very easy to be made and you can gain a lot of energy while you are eating them. You can have all the amount of relish while you eat them and you are able to get away from the stubbornness that your body takes. Plus, these chips also contain a sliced portion of fruits for you. Fruits, coupled with salad can be very productive for your health. In this way, you can achieve all the accumulation of enjoyment that you can get.

3. Green Apple Slices with Raw almond butter

An almond contains infinite pieces of energy for your body and you can get all amount of relish while eating them. While green apple slices are available in all ranges and prices for you, the almonds that you will add in them will create another tone for you. These green apples are sliced, which means that it can create a taste of juice for you. With almond butter, you have an intake of amino acids for you and thus, this diet can serve as a total package. All you need to do is to follow the regulations while creating it and you can end being very popular in your locality.

4. Apple Cabbage Salad with Beetroot

A crunchy salad for you, which is very ketogenic in its nature and can be helpful throughout the year; it has an easy process of its making. You need an apple, a cabbage, tomatoes and green leaves for. The beetroot is able to condense the fat intake in proper chemicals that can be helpful for you. You can stay alert in your busy routine throughout the year and you can get all the amount of relishes for yourself. You are able to give proper satisfaction to your clients any way in your duty. This diet can reduce the amount of acidity with full intellect and zeal. You are able to strive for excellence and betterment in all ways possible. You feel great and have a decent amount of excellency in your lifestyle.

5.   Zucchini Sushi

If you are a sushi lover and want to maintain a ketogenic state of your body then zucchini sushi is the real deal for you. You can get all the possibilities of relishes while making it and your body will be able to perform well. You can also do the filling for yourself and can in time, be very healthy while doing it. The dip of it is super flavorful and you can get the taste of it in all possible ways. The ingredients for this diet are four zucchinis, a quarter cup of parsley, I artichoke hearts, two cloves of garlic, one lemon, which is fresh juices and one can of white beans. You can slice the juicy zucchini in all the possible directions and mix the ingredients for a healthy amount of processing in it. You can also spread the zucchini for all the possible taste and can get satisfaction for it.

6.   Courgetti and Quinoa Salad

The ingredients of this salad are very healthy for our body. These are washed and sliced courgettes. These are one cup quinoa, one cup cumin, one tin chickpeas, which are rinsed well and drained, one garlic clove, which is crushed with sea salt, three tablespoons of extra virgin oil, two tablespoons are lemon juice, two spring onions that are chopped properly and small handful flat-leaf parsley leaves. The method to create such a diet is also very impressive. Add the quinoa to a pot, add a cup of water, bring to the boil over medium heat and then simmer it for ten minutes until all the water is properly absorbed. Replace the lid and make all the ingredients mix with it properly. After doing it, heat the olive oil in a large pan. Addition of courgettes is the next step. Cook with the stirring until bright green and tender spoon. Spoon it into a bowl, season and set aside. Replace the pan over medium heat; add the cumin and heat, stirring until fragrant. In the last step, add the spiced oil to the courgettes.

In the last add the chickpeas, quinoa, garlic, extra virgin oil, lemon juice, spring onions, and parsley and toss them well.

7. Cauliflower Gnocchi

This diet is very vegan and great in its formation. The ingredients include one head of cauliflower, one cloves of garlic, one cup of flour, one tablespoon of olive, one tin of white tomatoes, five courgettes of thickly sliced salads, half onions that are finely sliced, one tablespoon of olive and coconut, two cloves of garlic, six large of mushrooms and three hundred milliliter of vegetable stock. You need to place the cauliflower and garlic in a food blender first. Then you must do a little smoothing. You must add a little salt odor to it as well. So, in this way, a protein-enriched ketogenic diet is at your service and it will yield many proper results as well.

8.   Kaule and cucumber kimchi

This green ketogenic diet is very beneficial and healthy for you. It gives you a great amount of protein, amino acids and triggers pro-active digestion in your body. Its ingredients are white cabbage, kale, which is chopped, sea salt, dried chili flakes, smoked paprika, garlic, ginger and a heavy dose of mineral water. You have to stir the ingredients properly. The squeezing of vegetables is very important and you can squeeze the vegetables for five minutes. With this method, natural water can easily come out of the vegetables and will provide a great amount of taste. The tips are as under: leave it on a kitchen counter, away from direct sunlight, next is the fermentation of the mixture for three weeks and then you are allowed to taste it. There are many tips while you prepare this dish. As this is the dish that required jars for your health, therefore; you can sterilize glass jars. For a hot mixture, the jar needs to be hot. This tip will impact the taste of the dish and will give you a crunchy taste in no time.

9. Cauliflower Tabbouleh Salad

This dish is very ketogenic for your health. The ingredients are one raw head of cauliflower, onion that should be chopped, flat-leaf parsley that must be 125 milliliters, 125 milliliters of mint, same amount of dint, cucumber, which must be finely diced, tomatoes should be there, and one small juice of lemon will add more taste, beef bangers, and fresh herb. The method is very crucial for you to understand. For having a tabbouleh salad, the cauliflower must be dried and washed properly. Cut the fish into chunks and add it into the food processor. The process is fine but it needs to be purified by all means necessary. For having a sausages flow, heat the pan over a pace of medium heat. Add a bit of olive oil for the taste and then dry the sausages for a proper taste. For fresh herbs, you need to add a group of dollops for a fresh and genuine taste.

10.   Grilled Courgette Salad

The best ketogenic dish that you can taste for a good relish and a healthy body is grilled courgette salad. It has a spicy list of ingredients that can be very helpful for human metabolism. The ingredients include six courgettes, eighty gram of watercress, sea salt, chili meant dressing, one red chili, and salt. For a better mechanism, the courgettes and watercress can be of high use. You have to slice the courgettes lengthwise, you must give a sprinkle of salts on the salads; do the dressing of salts, wash the lemon, mint leaves, and chili while having a salad make, place the watercress in the serving dish and create more flavor in it by having additional tastes for it. Once you have done all it then you can do the dressing part effectively.

11.   Roasted Vegetable Oil and Coconut Milk soup

This vegetable ketogenic diet is very vane for you. Having ketogenic diets in it gives this dish a very proper and genuine taste. The ingredients of this diet include two shopped vegetables, olive oil, which is used to roast vegetables, salt, and black pepper to taste, one tablespoon of butter, one freshly grated ginger and salt and pepper for a taste. First and foremost, you need to heat it over 180 degrees Celsius; you have to arrange the chopped vegetables in a regular manner, you can add the butter and saute the garlic and ginger, you may also add the coconut milk and simmer it for thirty minutes, once this is done you can transfer coconut milk to a bowl and add vegetables to it. These tactics will help to ensure the taste you desire in the diet.

12.   Crunchy quinoa salad

This crunchy quinoa salad is very good and delicious for your healthy state of mind. Without its use, the autophagy of the body can be easily processed. The ingredients of the salad contain raw quinoa, raw butternut, raw cauliflower, olive oil, cucumber, raw carrot, kale, mint, Danish feta, pumpkin seeds, salt and pepper, lemon vinaigrette, wholegrain mustard, and parsley. These dishes can be very helpful for you as they give enough taste and autophagy in the body. All such tactics require a sheer sense of mixing and food dynamics and one should always abide by the notion of cleanliness first. In a frying pan, you need to heat a little olive oil. Pan Fry cauliflower until they are colored. You need to place all vinaigrette ingredients into a jug blender and blend them together.

Also, mix them with lemon vinaigrette and toss them upside down.

Thus, these lunch recipes will serve the taste of ketogenic lunch recipes for you and you will get all the relish and quality of freshness while you are eating it.

Dinner Recipes

We all want a satisfying and delicious dinner that can end our routines and also the dinner that gives us less fat while we are sleeping. For such dinners, we have to search and must come up with autophagy in them. These are the dinners which will make your bodies look lean and aesthetic. These recipes along with their mechanisms are as follows:

1. Brilliant Beet Lattles

Beet lattles can be very helpful for your bodies as they provide enormous impacts of energies. If you add a pouring of almond milk in the lattle, it will be very helpful for you. You have to be quite specific in this regard. The beet lattle is very colorful and it is also creamy. The creation of this epic diet is very easy. You need to follow all the mechanism related to it. The mechanism involves tenacious workings. It starts with the pouring of two almond kinds of milk into the blender; for this purpose, you have to use strained milk. Then you add some preferred sweetener to it. The sweetener can be dates or birch xylitol to it. After the addition of two teaspoons of beet powder, vanillas extract and ginger to it. Then is the use of high-speed blender that gives a friction heat of blades to the public. Secure the lid of the blender and then start to mix it up. However, if you are using a conventional machine then you have to give more mixing to the ingredients.

This single beet powder can be of very uses. The first use is in an almond milk latte, boost the content and nutrient content of smoothies, give more taste to raw alkalis, also in smoothies and workload, and you may add color to the pancakes as well if you are using the beetles. Also, there is a pasta flavor to it. There can be a gorgeous color to the salads and also, there can be a natural food coloring to the toy dough as well.

Beet lattle has a lot of health benefits as well. It is loaded with vitamins, minerals, antioxidants, dietary fiber, and nutrients. This compound, which is ketogenic in its nature can give stronger blood regulations, can give cellular healing, can give oxygen uptake, improves stamina and tries to give endurance for any mechanical workouts.

2.   Gluten-Free Vegan Berry Pie

This pie is a great deal for tonight. As it has all the important requirements that a body needs to get before sleep. It has minerals, proteins and juicy vitamins, which can yield the proper amount of energy for your body. It has a great way of formation. Its mechanism includes the chilling of work bowl in your freezer, wrap your flour packet in a plastic bag, storing it in the freezer, the keeping of fats and at the end, sweeten your fruit for your own good. While sweetening the pie, there are certain modes of it. You have to follow the processing of blueberries, the intake of Marionberries, the use of cherries and the chemical of rhubarb. These experiments help you to give a good dinner ketogenic food that is great for your body. Also, it eliminates any rusted pieces of fat that are present in the body.

3.   Spicy Cashew Tip

A beautiful, rich and creamy texture is all that you will find in the diet and form of spicy cashew tip. It is very fantastic when it comes to serving it at dinner. It is revered by all the families here and there and it gives a great tone of affection when it is served on the table.

You can also do the creamy salad dressing on your foods through the spicy cashew tip. There are many bursting flavors at the core of this diet and it helps to regain a lot of taste in your body while you eat them. The dish is inspired by the Indian Recipes like the potato and cauliflower curry, the spicy aloo gobi, okra masala, and banana cardamom lassi. These are the diets and recipes that can be used in many ways to keep your sleep ketogenic. The autophagy is therefore reserved in these products and you can come up with many other credentials as well.

These are the dinner recipes that give a ketogenic taste to your body. You must try your best in eating and preserving them.

Chapter 6 - Autophagy for muscle mass

Intermittent fasting

The concept of intermittent fasting means that you have to fast at regular intervals of the daily routine. The autophagy works tremendously under such circumstances and with the passage of time, the working length can be achieved mordaciously. However, there are certain techniques that need to be compensated while you are doing intermittent fasting. They are as follows:

1. The ketosis states

It is a state of intermittent fasting in which the body is able to lower down its metabolic rate and all the saturated fats, located in various parts of the body are easily eliminated. You tend to start this while you are at the 12th hour of your body level and this state forces you to be away from all those bad things that are quite hectic for your body. You become all composed and compassionate in your self while you are at this diet and thus, you are all good to come and proceed in the coming.

2. The recycling of cells

During the second state of the body, the body is able to do the recycling of cells. The cell line is so lenient and efficient in this scenario that you become very effective in this regard. The recycling of cells is an autophagy process and helps to improve the circulation of blood in your holistically. Therefore, the use of autophagy is tremendously very effective for your body to work on and with this, you are able to make a better transition in your body by all means necessary.

3. The 54 hours shift

By this state, the insulin level has dropped by 54 percent and you are feeling very relaxed and better in your style. This the hours' shift that helps you to lessen any composed fat on your waistline and with the passage of time, you are able to be very strong and sustainable in your requirement. Therefore, these three stages are a must to learn states of intermittent fasting and anyone, who desires to have an autophagy run in it, the 54 hours shift is the best shift for it.

Incorporating intermittent fasting

In order to incorporate intermittent fasting in you. You have to adopt the following things in yourself.

1. Be patient and composed

This means that any diet that has a good number of intakes in it and can deliver a better potential in you with the passage of time, it is essential and effective for you. The idea in this scenario is that you have to look for diet and body ideas that can be helpful for you in a coherent level and could engage the best out of you. This might be a little problematic at first but with the passage of time, you will be able to harness it.

2. Always look for a green diet

The green diet will help you to pay a better benefit to your body. You will be able to see how the body language is able to incorporate better standings in you and with the passage of time, you are able to furnish yourself to the next level. Therefore, it is important for you to understand that looking for a green diet for you is the best thing ever happen to you and you must incorporate it in the coming time.

Into your workout plan

The keto diet and the process of autophagy should be incorporated in your work out plan. You must be able to see how the work out is able to make you stand out in front of any issue. You must incorporate physical exercises that could be very effective for your brain and could make you very established in physique as well. Therefore, the incorporation of a workout plan is necessary for you to understand how the body is being moved with possible direction and how autophagy can help to relate in this manner.

Chapter 7 Foods that stimulate autophagy

Following are some of the foods that stimulate autophagy

Ginger

Ginger is a food that stimulates autophagy ghastly and makes things come close in an effective manner.

Green Tea

Green tea is the best drinking lot that can help you to be lean and adopt autophagy in you. It has some herbs and essential ingredients that are designed to give better illustrations to the people. The green tea is easy to mix and can be capitalized easily in the coming time. The green tea requires no such working in the products and can be available in every possible direction

Reishi Mushrooms

Reishi mushrooms can be easily accepted in the world timings and these mushrooms could be made out of nowhere. The mushrooms make the body language more lenient in its desire and with the passage of time, the people are able to learn a lot from its core and construct. The constructs of the mushrooms need to be identified with the passage of time and they are best to carry out an autophagy product.

Turmeric/curcumin

Turmeric is a regimental disease that could be very healthy and compatible with autophagy. It does not require a lot of working for its process and it could easily up bring the concept of better regulations in the time. Therefore, the turmeric and curcumin are the best details looking forward to the people in the society.

Chapter 8 - Stimulating Autophagy by mimicking food

Example of a Fasting-Mimicking diet protocol

Some meat plans are offered in this scenario to make the reader know about the formation of a fast mimicking diet

Basics of the fasting-mimicking diet and its importance in lifestyle

First, let us discuss what is meant by a lifestyle? The lifestyle of an individual is based on his daily routine, his calorie intake, his daily processions, and the repute; he carries along with him while pursuing the daily lifestyle. The lifestyle of a starlet can be very famous. He will ride new vehicles; he will look healthy and try his best to do the best in his movies. He will professionalize his life by working hard and he will adopt a healthy regime in his routine to be successful.

Therefore, the daily choices, in terms of food, clothing and routine procession, a lifestyle can be defined.

Now why the alkaline lifestyle is so popular? What basic ingredients, it holds in it that makes it famous. The result of having a fast mimicking diet is very successful in its reflection and the confidence that any individual can harness through it is the real reason why the intake of a fast mimicking diet can be very effective. People deem it famous because they become famous or at-least become renowned to the fact that they are in the limelight. The idea of popularity can be assessed through this notion that eating a fast mimicking diet can make you fit and being fit, can be the source of a healthy lifestyle. While having a lifestyle, you can do a lot of works, a lot of practice and can execute many frameworks through effective planning. This argument can be further prolonged to many levels of analysis.

The first level of analysis is the individualistic level. On an individualistic level, individuals get revered to be the lean and muscular figures that have the potential to succeed in life. They can do a lot of things like move composedly in their professional careers, they can be the focus on their diets and prevent their bodies from being affected by many health diseases like TB, heart cancer, kidney stone and even fracture of bones. They can go to popular lifestyles like the fashion industry and even apply for acting careers. Therefore, on an individualistic level, one can easily transform the credentials of his self into a famous personality. All he needs to do is to have a fast mimicking diet in his routine.

On a social level, a society steams into the portions of activeness and recognition through a fast mimicking diet. A society is able to get all the intention and popularity if it follows a fast mimicking diet because the functions of society and the correlation of social institutions can be effective in their progress and allowing the intake of a fast mimicking diet will always open a plethora of opportunities for the society to flourish in the status-quo. Also, the norms and values are equally translated into the successful sustenance of any society and the claws of societal decadence are easily averted. So, on a societal level, there are many features of having a fast mimicking diet that can be very helpful for a society to boost its formation in the contemporary. All the societies, whether western or eastern, must be allowed to have a taste of this fast mimicking diet and this diet could be effective for the nourishment of their lifestyles.

The state-level can also be analyzed while discussing the popularity of a fast mimicking diet. The state is an engine for any country's progress and without its efficient working and statehood; a nation cannot become successful in geopolitics and geo-economics. Leaders need to adopt a fast mimicking diet system that can be healthy for their country's lead and they can steer the nation's ship with productive body metabolisms. For instance, the food regimen of China's President, Mr. Xi Jinping is of significance. The guy does not claim to have a fast mimicking diet but still, his bodily gestures coupled with prudent state policies make him be a decisive state man. Also, there are many leaders that abhor such a food style and hence, the leaders of a state, if they are using an alkaline, they become popular while exhibiting an alkaline lifestyle.

Thus, the modes of working, daily routines and lifestyle are all affected by the proper intake of a fast mimicking diet. Hence, on a social, individualistic and state level, the use of a fast mimicking diet can trigger many bodily changes in a human body and this is all the cause of the popularity of a fast mimicking diet.

Day one

For day one, the following description must be followed to get a comprehensive change to a body.

1. Breakfast

Breakfast will be strawberry cocoa chia quinoa. The ingredients for this breakfast are one cup cooked quinoa, two dates, five chia seeds, almond pieces, one-half cup of almond, coconut or hemp milk, coconut shredded flakes, four sliced strawberries and a half cup of almond. The direction will be impact-full if you follow it with strict rules. The night before you cook quinoa, you have to be very diligent. Cook quinoa and strawberry chia before cooking the quinoa and mix the strawberries, almond milk and two dates in a blender. Puree them until they are smoothed. Pour the mixture of the jar and add chia seeds to it. You have to do the mixing until all the seeds are covered with milk. Cover it with the lid and refrigerate overnight. In the morning, when you wake up you must place chia seeds in a bowl and add the quinoa in a homogeneous manner. Enjoy the shredded coconut and serve it to your meal.

2. Lunch

Lunch will be the sweet and savory salad. The ingredients are one large head of butter lettuce, cucumber sliced, cup apple vinegar, one pomegranate, extra virgin oil, one avocado cubed, one garlic clove and quarter cup shelled pistachios. The directions for this recipe are: You have to hand and tear the lettuce in a salad bowl and then add the rest of the ingredients.

Day two

The following description should be kept in mind while following the plan on day two.

1. Breakfast

Breakfast will be a nondairy apple parfait. Ingredients contain half cup-soaked cashews, one cup chopped apple, half cup unsweetened almond or coconut milk and vanilla. Directions contain the combinations of cashews, almond milk, and vanilla in a blender and their blending until you smooth them. The layering of the ingredients in a small cup is the next step. Heaping of the spoon of cashew cream and dressing the top with oats must be there to see the finish the diet.

2. Lunch

Lunch will be a savory avocado wrap. The ingredients for this recipe are one butter lettuce, one tablespoon of cilantro, half of the avocado, quarter red onion, one tablespoon of chopped basil, a small handful of spinach and sea salt and pepper. Direction includes the spreading the avocado onto a leaf and sprinkle the dish with salt, basil, cilantro, red onion, and spinach. This final dressing will be pertinent to ensure the taste of the dish in all the possible directions.

Day three

In the third day, following recipes need to be followed:

1. Breakfast

Breakfast will be an almond butter crunch berry smoothie. The ingredients will be two cups fresh spinach, one banana, two cup almond milk, four raw almond butter, one cup of any of strawberries, grapes and mixed berries. One tablespoon of chia. Directions include the blending of spinach and almond first milk. Add remaining ingredients except for chia and blend it in. Add more chia once the mixture is all smooth. If you do not possess a valuable speed blender then you must mix more chai in the ingredients. Just sit for a moment and enjoy it with full esteem.

2. Lunch

Lunch will be kale pesto pasta in this scenario. Its ingredients include one bunch kale, sea salt, and pepper, two cups fresh basil, one zucchini, which is noodled, a quarter cup of extra virgin oil, half cup walnuts, garnish with sliced asparagus, spinach leaves, and tomato, two limes and fresh sprinklers of salt. Directions are very pertinent to follow when there are such recipes to eat. In the night, you need to soak walnuts to give absorption. Put all ingredients in the blender or food processor, and blend it until you get cream of consistency. In the end, add some zucchini noodles.

Day four

The following description must be added to witness the intake on day four.

1. Breakfast

Breakfast will be apple and almond butter oats. The ingredients will be two cups of gluten-free oats, one cup grated green apple, half cup of coconut oil, one teaspoon of cinnamon and one by three raw almond butter. The directions include the addition of oats, coconut milk, and almond butter into a bowl and mix well. After it, stir the mixture in the mixture in the grated apple, cover the bowl with a lid or plastic wrap and place it in the refrigerator. Refrigerate overnight. If the oats get too thick, add some coconut milk to like them. In the end, garnish the mixture with cinnamon powder.

2. Lunch

Lunch will be Green Goddess bowl with avocado cumin dressing. Ingredients are divided into different dressings. The first dressing is for avocado cumin dressing. Ingredients include the presence of one avocado, one cumin powder, two limes, one cup filtered water, quarter tablespoon sea salt, extra virgin oil, dash cayenne pepper, a quarter of smoked paprika. The other dressing is the ingredients are for Tahini Lemon Dressing. The ingredients include a quarter cup of tahini, half cup of filtered water, half lemon, which is freshly squeezed, one clove minced garlic, quarter sea salt, dash cayenne pepper, smoked paprika, black pepper to taste and minced garlic. The other layer is for salad. Ingredients include three cups kale, half cup key noodles, half cup broccoli florets, cherry tomatoes, half zucchini, and hemp seeds. The directions of this lunch recipe are lightly steamed kale and broccoli for four minutes, mix zucchini noodles, kelp noodles, toss with a generous serving of smoked avocado and have a cumin dressing. Add cherry tomatoes in it and toss them again. Next, you need to plate the steamed kale and broccoli and try to drizzle them with lemon tahini dressing. Top kale and broccoli with the dressed noodles and tomatoes. In the end, sprinkle the whole dish and hemp them with seeds.

Day five

The description is composed of the following diets

1. Breakfast

For breakfast, we have the berry good spinach power smoothie. The ingredients for this recipe are two cups of fresh spinach, one coconut oil, two cups of unsweetened almond milk, one tablespoon of cinnamon, one cup from mixed berries, one raw almond butter and one frozen banana. The direction is that you need to blend spinach and almond milk first then you can add the remaining ingredients to the mixture.

2. Lunch

Lunch, in this scenario, will be a quinoa burrito bowl. The ingredients for this recipe include the cup of quinoa, four garlic cloves, two hundred and fifteen cans of black beans, one heaping cumin, four green onions sliced, two avocados sliced and two limes fresh juiced. The direction in this recipe will be the cooking of quinoa to get a good shape of quinoa. Then you have to warm the beans for your intake. When quinoa is done cooking then you have to divide the mixture in various serving bowls. You need to top with beans, avocado, and cilantro.

Day six

This day will have the following recipes to start with.

1. Breakfast

Breakfast will be quinoa morning porridge. The ingredients will contain a half cup of rinsed quinoa, chia seeds, can of coconut milk, hemp seeds, and cinnamon. The direction will be the combination of all the ingredients except the hemp seeds and simmer them for 10-15 minutes until liquid is absorbed. Sprinkle them with hemp seeds.

2. Lunch

Lunch will be thai quinoa salad. The ingredients for dressing will be chopped seeds, cup tahini, lemon-fresh juiced, one pitted date, one teaspoon of apple cider vinegar, one salt, one tamari, and gluten-free and toasted sesame oil. Ingredients for salad will be one cup of quinoa steamed, one tomato sliced, one large handful of arugula and a quarter of red onion sliced. Directions include the blending of all the following, filtered water first and then the rest of all the ingredients. Then you can blend them. After it, you have to steam one cup of quinoa in a steamer or rice cooker and then you can set aside things. Combination of all the quinoa, arugula, sliced tomatoes, diced red onion, onto a serving plate and bowl and then add thai dressing and hand mix with a spoon and serve.

Day seven

The description is as follows for this day.

1. Breakfast

Breakfast will be an alkaline warrior chia breakfast. The ingredients are one cup of unsweetened almond or coconut milk, one tablespoon of unsweetened shredded coconut flakes, four tablespoons of chia seeds, vanilla, cinnamon, chopped nuts, and hemp seeds. The direction includes a combination of milk and chia seeds in a mason jar. Add vanilla, cinnamon, and chopped nuts. Then you can cover the lid with the mixture until it is combined. Refrigerate the mixture overnight. The next morning shake it or stir it with two or three bowls. Top it with optional fresh fruit, coconut shreds, and more chopped fruits.

2. Lunch

Lunch will be the Asian Sesame dressing and noodles. The ingredients will include two tablespoons of tahini, one tamari, liquid coconut nectar, lemon-fresh squeeze, and ingredients will be one scallion, one tablespoon raw sesame seeds, sliced red bell pepper, and carrot. The direction for the lunch will be the choice of either chopping the noodles or using a zucchini. In a mixing bowl, combine all the dressing ingredients and thoroughly mix the spoon. Make your zucchini noodles with a spiralizer or if using kelp noodles, place in warm water for ten minutes to rinse off the liquid, they are packaged with, allowing them to separate and soften. Add the Asian sesame for your dressing and mix it thoroughly. You will have a great amount of relish and comfort for your digestion.

Follow a similar plan for the remaining twenty-three days. The entire meal plan has to be similar to an equal amount of intake and balance. The dinner can be any from the dinner recipes and try your best in maintaining a lesser intake of dinner.

Day Eight

The description is as follows for this day.

1. Breakfast

Breakfast will be French toast. The ingredients are bread, egg and heating pan. You need to careful while padding the bread in the jar. The direction includes a combination of milk and chia seeds in a mason jar. Add vanilla, cinnamon and chopped nuts for a good flavor. Then you can cover the lid with the mixture until it is combined. Refrigerate the mixture overnight. The next morning shake it or stir it with two or three bowls. Top it with optional fresh fruit, coconut shreds, and more chopped fruits.

2. Lunch

Lunch will be the summer salad with citrus dressing. Salads make a fantastic lunch and if you dress them with juices and sprinkle salts on them then they can make good use of the health as well. You have to do all the cutting and dressing and must try your best in getting the greenish salads for your own benefit. You can only reap benefits for yourself if you are able to amalgamate tomatoes, carrots, green-left, cabbage and lemons in the salad. For a salty taste, you can sprinkle some salads on the salad for your own relish. This meal is very conducive for your health and can be used in many situations while you want a lunch meal for you. You have to very keen while looking at this situation and you will get all the amazing results to your body if you have a salad for yourself.

Day Nine

The description is as follows for this day.

1. Breakfast

Apple pancakes are the great treasury for you if you strive for an alkaline diet. This diet is recommended by the entire in all ifs and buts of life. A beautiful mixing of apples in sweat odors of a cake is essential for its making. With a cup of tea, apple pancakes are the healthiest autophagy of all. Also, these pancakes are very easy to make and they can be given in all ranges of prices to the customers. For its making, you need a half cup of flour, a half teaspoon of grounded cinnamon, an egg whisked, one-third cup full of milk, two red apples, cooking oil, blueberries and low-fat frozen yogurt. With these ingredients, the apple pancakes can be easily made and there is a lot of delicious taste attached to it.

2. Lunch

These kips contain all the necessary amounts of minerals, amino acids, proteins, and enzymes the human body needs. They are very easy to be made and you can gain a lot of energy while you are eating them. You can have all the amount of relish while you eat them and you are able to get away from the stubbornness that your body takes. Plus, these chips also contain a sliced portion of fruits for you. Fruits, coupled with salad can be very productive for your health. In this way, you can achieve all the accumulation of enjoyment that you can get.

Day ten

The description is as follows for this day.

1.   Breakfast

The breakfast will be the avocado salad. This breakfast salad can help you regain all your lost energies in you when you are sleeping. It is the Mexican salad that can help you give important details to your intake at all the possible levels of your body. Its ingredients are two tortillas, half a spoon of firm tofu, one avocado, a handful of almonds, one spoon of chili sauce, half a red onion and half a lemon. Its make is very simple as well and every layman, who wants a fast and healthy diet, can use this salad for its own making.

2. Lunch

Lunch will be green almond slices with rich grains. An almond contains infinite pieces of energy for your body and you can get all amount of relish while eating them. While green apple slices are available in all ranges and prices for you, the almonds that you will add in them will create another tone for you. These green apples are sliced, which means that it can create a taste of juice for you. With almond butter, you have an intake of amino acids for you and thus, this diet can serve as a total package. All you need to do is to follow the regulations while creating it and you can end being very popular in your locality.

These ten meal day plans will ensure fasting-mimicking in your body in a longer span of time.

Chapter 9 - 10 tips to help with fasting

Following are the fresh ten tips to help with fasting

1. Eat fresh

Whenever you want better food for yourself or would want to come up with fasting then you have to start eating fresh. Eating fresh means that all those herbal diets that are available for you must be taken for food installments.

2. Have a clear-sighted goal for eating

While eating never eat junk or bad food just to see how it is. Avoid it at all possible rates.

3. Keep on moving and never stop it

While fasting, belly fat can become a trouble for it. Belly fat becomes stubborn belly fat because it does not get melted. You are sitting and eating and you are gaining much fat without knowing it. What happens is that while sitting and doing no physical exertion, you are gaining visceral fat and the unnecessary fat keeps on improving at your waist. When you will exercise or at least walk or run, you will get a sweat on your belly. The repeated movements will melt the stubborn fat in no time.

4. Load up more proteins

Once you get old, your body produces insulin. Insulin helps gain fat faster and it provides vast storage for fats in the body. Women, who get older and who do not maintain a diet, they feel fat because their bodies do not have a balanced diet. They do not eat vegetables, beef or any other substance that offers proteins and instead they compile a lot of fat on their waist. Hence, more protein than fat should be eaten to maintain a balanced diet in your body.

5. Pile on Polyunsaturates

Saturated fats give more fats as compare to polyunsaturated fats. According to a Swedish study, when individuals eat food either in the form of saturated oil or unsaturated oil than the former gives more weight to the client as the latter one. The saturated oils give a boost to visceral fats on the body while the polyunsaturated ones give less weight and energy to the fat. This is for both men and women to study the significance of polyunsaturated and they should use them in their cooking.

6. Sleep early

While you are fasting, try your best in sleeping early. This will help you to get to the best fasting regimen easily. The fasting comes with a strong viewpoint of things properly and with the passage of time, the people are able to have a better style of it in their characters for fasting. Fasting comes with all the pieces and products effectively and therefore, sleeping is a process that can make the neutral of the body closely and energetically. Therefore, do your best in sleeping early and never hesitate while you are fasting.

7. Avoid smoking at all cost

Smoking is injurious to health. It's painful as it drains all the useful vitamins from the body and if done vigorously, can cause lung fatigue, heart failure, anxiety and many other bodily diseases. Out of the total population of the world, seventy-five-person daily smoke and thirty-five of them are prone to heart diseases and other body malfunctions. This is a serious issue and many countries have formulated an anti-smoking policy among adolescents just to cater to the outcomes of smoking. However, in order to dilute the harmful effects of smoking, a process has been introduced called smoking cessation. This article shall discuss the meaning of smoking cessation and its benefits.

Smoking cessation is a process in which the tobacco content of the cigarette is removed for healthy purposes. It also involves behavioral counseling and communicating in a productive manner. Other cessation techniques include dilution in selling cigarettes and approaching the victim in a positive manner. There are 5a's in the smoking cessation process that are asked, advise, assess, assist and arrange. In asking, a person is inquired of the reason why he/she is smoking and further motivation is given to rectify the menace. In advice, the victim is encouraged to quit the smoke and start doing a healthy activity in the coming time. Assessment involves the mental study of the victim's body and how he can be shaped back to normal. Assistance is the motivation given to the victim so that he may come back to the normal state at the earliest. At last, the arrangement is the process of organizing sustainable livelihoods for the victim and giving him/her an emotional asylum to carry on life for a better purpose.

Smoking cessation has many benefits as well. During the process of 5a's, the endeavor elevates the political, social and economic condition of the victim and helps him to regain his life's objectives in a resonant manner. Furthermore, he is given the motivation to sustain his life for better purposes. Distance from smoking impedes the addiction in a person's mind and abates any bodily disease in him. Once the disease is finished and exterminated, normal metabolism rises in the human body and he can do any tasks in a courageous manner. Thereby smoking cessation guarantees a healthy life possible at all outcomes and it furnishes a stable mechanism for all the human beings involved in the process.

Moving forward, smoking cessation is vital to form a strong family bond. Often in addition, the victim tends to isolate himself from the family closure. He feels distant from the family's affiliation and has no inner love for the family's responsibilities. Smoking cessation does the miracle for him and nurtures him for the best in the coming time.

8. Never exercise while on a fast

Do not do exercises while you are on fast as the body system will lose its stamina and will make you look very bad in its comprehension.

9. Never argue with anyone

Do not argue with anyone who is not in a good mode of yourself. The very better place for it is that you have to be very complacent with others and try to have a better fast.

10. Always be positive.

Positivity comes with a strong impression of being in a relationship and while on fast do your best in refraining from any agitation.

Chapter 10 - Tips to help you optimize autophagy

For optimization of autophagy you have to be the following

1. Eat medicines that are hydrated
2. Never argue with anyone as it increases blood cholesterol
3. Always look for good modes
4. Avoid fats and lipids
5. Eat a healthy diet
6. Be honored to have a doctor visit your place
7. The idea of rationality
8. Never fell guilty pleasure of eating fast foods
9. Always research on your body and have good relationships with others
10. Have an immense load of food intake in you
11. Never underestimate the power of suggestions

Conclusion

To conclude the book, you have to be very careful about diet intakes that you do throughout your routine. You need to be curious about every calorie that goes in you. You have been provided with all the reasons in this book about the process of autophagy. Autophagy can give you a healthy ph and can avert any harmful stroke of acidity in the body. Acidity can be dangerous in profuse accumulation fats, rise to inflammatory disease, the rupture in many digestion organs and having a rusted metabolism that does not work in the flow. On the contrary, autophagy can give you a fresh intake of all healthy diets that can be very healthy and caring for you. These diets are present in all formats.

They are in breakfast recipes, the dinner recipes, the lunch recipes, the smoothies and the sweat desserts that can up-satisfaction in your mouth. You do not have to be an expert in medicine to know which diet to follow when. You just have to know the diet intake of your own body and see how you are able to cater to the plight of diseases. You must not be able to compound yourself with the attack of acidity but must have the courage to use these diets and recover at the earliest.

These diets have everything in their DNA. They have the minerals, the enzymes, the protein, the amino acids, and whatnot. Green refluxes along with curing liquids are present in these diets and they come in all whims and fancies of the diet expression. There is no rocket science behind their creation and one has to be very intelligent while creating them. You can also follow this book and will get a splendid amount of results in no time. It is available at an affordable price.

Try your best in avoiding any acidic diet at all costs even if it gives you a great amount of relish. The idea is fats and minerals are very delicious but they come with devious outcomes of fat accumulation and strengths.

You need to understand that long aging is only possible if you have a balanced diet intake and this diet can be only of an alkaline.

To make conclusive remarks of the book about the benefits of an alkaline diet, first and foremost is the sheer activeness that a person tends to achieve while he is eating an alkaline diet. He feels healthy and looks healthy and wants to be doing a lot of things while he is having an alkaline diet. He can think properly and can get rid of inflammatory diseases that can cause him suffering. He has a strong discipline that can be navigated in any way possible and thus, he is the next big thing for his users. Also, the longevity of life in this scenario and truly, autophagy can do a lot of wonders for the individual. Therefore, autophagy has a lot to do for fitness and active-ness in the human body.

Furthermore, If you want to look green and fresh on your face, then the autophagy can be very helpful in this regard. Studies show that autophagy is very popular in making a healthy face for you. The number of herbs and breakfast recipes you have for yourself, up-bring a good amount of freshness on your face as well on your skin. Thus, autophagy is very crucial for having great skin and face.

Autophagy protects bone density and muscle mass. The mineral intake that you get after having autophagy can protect your bone density. The bones need certain minerals that are used to cure the excessive number of hurdles one gets while running. The minerals are given by autophagy and you are able to get a stronger bone for life. If you are a bodybuilder and want to reap the benefits of the bone then you have to accumulate more autophagy in you that can be very beneficial for you. The muscle mass can be secured in an acute manner if you tend to get more and more almonds and other alkaline dietaries. You have to be very lenient when you are having the autophagy because the benefit of autophagy like the muscle mass and the bone density will be instrumental for you. Just always look at the bright side of the diet and you will feel very productive while you do it.

In today's world, tensions are like a haunting disease that wants to remain at your back for no reason. Everywhere you go, you get a tertiary level of tension. There is the tension of graduating, the tension of succeeding in life, the tension of getting a job and tension of whatnot. You believe that tension can be very successive for you but in the latter, it turns out to be adverse. Scientists have claimed very medical drugs for its cure but the only reasonable cure for is the use of an alkaline diet. The enzymes that you get through vegetables lower the risk of your hyper blood tension and then you can achieve all the relish of your lifestyle in no time. Also, your blood level starts to resonate with full capacity and you will feel like a superman every place you go, therefore; hypertension and tensed matters get an upper hand of resolution when you get to know the prospect of an alkaline diet.

You are able to get a lot of chronic pains in your body due to many reasons. You get to the bottom of any problem; you solve it and end up having chronic pain in your body. Chronic pain refers to any tertiary amount of pain in your body and you are able to get to the harmfulness of it in no time. Therefore, chronic pain is the most devastating headache that you can get and the only effective cure of it is the alkaline diet. Yes, the autophagy is very important for you to maintain as the blood level minimizes when lemon or other alkaline water is induced in the body. So, this is another benefit of autophagy and it does not matter if you are a walker, a boxer or even a corporate worker, you must have autophagy in you if you wish to give all that you crave.

In the end, we will only assure you good health and being a beginner, you must waste any further time and order this book in a jiffy. Because health is wealth nobody became rich while being lazy and stubborn. This book is all that you need and you must get at all costs.